Buddhist Origami
The Ancient Art of Mindful Paper-Folding

Table of Contents

Chapter 1. Introduction

Welcome to a voyage of serene tranquility and reflection, unraveling a unique nexus between traditional Buddhist teachings and the art of origami. In this special report, "Buddhist Origami: The Ancient Art of Mindful Paper-Folding," we explore not only the process of transforming a plain sheet of paper into a beautiful shape but also the inner transformation that occurs when your mind is immersed in the calm and focus of this ancient practice. We will bring into light how this art form can be a gateway to mindfulness, meditation, and even stimulate insights about the Buddhist philosophy. If you ever wanted an enlightening and serene hobby, join us on this journey. This report has it all - it is an origami manual, a beginner's guide to Buddhism and a testament to the power of mindfulness, all woven intricately into an incredible narrative that's guaranteed to captivate. Don't wait to take the first step into a realm where tranquility meets creativity; secure your copy today!

Chapter 2. The Intersection of Buddhism and Origami: An Intriguing History

In the ancient times of the 6th century BCE, marked by the birth of Buddha, the world began to hum with the echoes of profound teachings about life, suffering, and the path to enlightenment. Almost concurrently, in the far-off land of China, the art of paper-folding began to take shape, eventually known as origami—a Japanese term that translates as 'folding (ori) + paper (gami)'.

This intriguing simultaneous emergence was no coincidence, it was the beginning of a mesmerizing intersection between Buddhism and origami.

2.1. The Birth of Buddhism and Origami

Buddhism started in the heart of India's Ganges plains around the 6th and 5th centuries BCE, with the enlightenment of Siddhartha Gautama, the Buddha. As the teachings spread across Asia, they influenced cultures and traditions, particularly in regions that welcomed Buddhism warmly, like Japan.

Origami too found its roots in the same era, in China, around the invention of paper. Initially, this art was reserved for ceremonial practices due to the high costs of paper production. However, as techniques developed and evolved, paper became cheaper and more accessible, and origami found its way into the hands of everyday people.

2.2. Buddhism's Arrival in Japan and the Spread of Origami

Buddhism arrived in Japan in the mid-6th century CE, and progressively influenced many aspects of Japanese society—the literature, the government, art, and various everyday rituals. Similarly, with the trade routes established between China and Japan, the practice and knowledge of paper-folding also traveled, entwining ultimately with Japanese culture.

The interconnected growth of Buddhism and origami in Japan is highly significant. As Buddhism's influences became integral to Japan's societal norms and behaviors, origami also evolved—going beyond simple amusement and taking on profound symbolic significance.

2.3. The Symbolism in Origami and Buddhist Philosophy

Origami is more than just an art of creating aesthetically pleasing figures out of paper—it is a practice imbued with intense symbolism that often mirrors Buddhist philosophies.

One of the most recognized symbols in origami is the crane. Known as the 'Orizuru', this sacred bird holds deep meaning in Japanese culture. It symbolizes hope, happiness, and a long life. It aligns with the Buddhist concept of the auspicious rebirth. Folding a thousand cranes is believed to make one's wish come true—representing humans' ability to shape their own destiny, a cornerstone idea in Buddhism.

Then, there's the origami lotus, a symbolic embodiment of the Buddhist notion of purity and rebirth—rising untainted and beautiful from the muddy waters. The process of shaping a simple piece of paper into the complex structure resonates with the journey towards enlightenment—the transformation from an ordinary human existence to the clarity and beauty of Buddha-nature.

2.4. Mindfulness, Meditation and Origami

While origami originated long before Buddhism's introduction in Japan, its ability to cultivate a sense of mindfulness and tranquility connects easily and profoundly with the Buddhist practice of meditation.

As one folds a piece of paper, one must pay complete attention to each crease, each turn, each transformation. This rapt focus fosters a sense of being in the present moment—a key aspect in the practice of mindfulness meditation.

Moreover, the process of origami encourages the individual to come into harmony with their inner self. As one folds paper, there is room for deep contemplation; one realizes the impermanence of things, another significant Buddhist teaching, as the paper evolves from one form to another and finally, to a piece of art.

2.5. Bridging the Gap Between the Ancient and the Modern

The parallels between Buddhism and origami have had a lasting impact on the Japanese and permeated into modern times, shaping cultural narratives and traditions while fostering mindfulness and creativity. An art form that began centuries ago alongside a profound philosophy, continues to thrive, entwining as a remarkable symbol of history, culture, and spiritual introspection.

Today, origami workshops are held in meditation retreats, Buddhist centers and schools to promote mindfulness and the connection one can find with the teachings of Buddha through the creative process.

2.6. Final Thoughts on The Intersection

The intersection of Buddhism and Origami is, without doubt, a beautiful illustration of how an art form and philosophy can blend seamlessly, co-exist, and accentuate each other in meaning and practice. This intertwining journey through time and culture, through folds and thoughts, helps make understanding Buddhist philosophy a more tangible, interactive experience—something you can touch, fold, unfold, and meditate upon.

And with each crease you make and every figure you bring to life, you embark on a parallel journey within yourself. The wisdom of Buddhism, the tranquility of meditation, and the creativity of origami—each twist, each fold, each transformation—offer a gateway to explorations not just of paper, but of the self, of life, and of the profound teachings that seek to bring peace to human existence. Today, even in the fast-paced world of the 21st century, this amalgamation of Buddhism and origami continues to hold its relevance, bequeathing artful mindfulness to those who tread its path.

Chapter 3. The Basics of Origami: Understanding Paper, Folds, and Shapes

As you unfold this chapter, it's important to begin your journey with a thorough understanding of the primary components essential to this craft: paper, folds, and shapes. The ancient art of origami springs from these three foundational elements, all coalescing together on an artist's hands to birth captivating creations.

3.1. The Right Paper

To start with origami, choosing the right kind of paper is crucial. While any type of paper can theoretically be transformed, not all types lend themselves ideally to the meticulous folding and unfolding this delicate craft demands.

The notion of 'right' paper varies, dynamic enough to change on factors such as the complexity of the model, the level of the artist, and the purpose of the creation. Here is a brief overview of the key forms of paper used in origami:

1. **Origami paper:** Probably the most common, this is thin and easy to fold, making it ideal for beginners. Available in a variety of different sizes and colors, it typically has a white reverse, highlighting the contrast in many models.

2. **Kami:** Of Japanese origin, Kami is a kind of affordable origami paper that comes in a rainbow of colors. It is slightly thicker than regular origami paper but is still relatively easy to work with.

3. **Tant:** Tant paper is a versatile type that comes in a large variety of colors. It's thicker than standard origami paper, making it appropriate for more complex models.

4. **Foil-backed paper:** This has a thin, shiny layer attached to one side of the paper. This metallic finish can make for some striking origami forms but it's worth noting that it can be trickier to work with for complex structures.

5. **Rice paper:** The malleability of rice paper makes it an excellent option for intricate, detailed models, yet it demands a higher level of skill.

3.2. The Mastery of Folds

Akin to the tones on a musician's palette or the brushstrokes of an artist, the diversity of origami folds acts as the lingua franca for origamists. Learning and mastering the basics is imperative to your evolution as an artist. Broadly, folds fall into two categories: simple folds and compound folds.

Simple folds are the most elementary, and the entire myriad of origami art is built on these basic structures:

1. **Valley fold (mountain reverse):** The most basic fold, it's akin to folding a piece of paper in half - the resulting 'valley' is the folded edge.

2. **Mountain fold (valley reverse):** The opposite of the valley fold, it results in a 'mountain'-like peak.

3. **Crimp fold:** A combination of one valley and one mountain fold.

4. **Pleat:** Multiple crimps in succession.

Compound folds are more complex, crafted by combining simple folds:

1. **Rabbit Ear:** It starts with two valley folds converging at a point, with a third valley fold bringing these together.

2. **Petal Fold:** A series of mountain and valley folds, reminiscent of a flowering petal.

3. **Kite Fold:** Formed by folding two edges inward to meet a central crease.

4. **Squash Fold:** This requires 'squashing' a flap of paper flat against itself.

3.3. Crafting Shapes and Models

Mastering folds allows one to craft shapes and models. These shapes evolve from multiple folds, each adding a layer of complexity to the model.

The first model every beginner learns is usually the traditional origami crane, or "Tsuru." Its elegant form shrouded in Japanese mythology is representative of health, prosperity, and luck. Other simple models for beginners might include the 'origami box' or 'origami jumping frog.'

With burgeoning confidence and growing competence in handling paper and mastering folds, you then progress to more complex models. There's an entire spectrum, from five-pointed stars, dragons, unicorns, and origami roses to complex geometric shapes like the intricately constructed modular 'Kusudama.'

One central philosophy in the sphere of origami is that every model, whether simple or sophisticated, is unique, bearing the signature of the artist's intent and the personal journey undertaken in its creation.

Herein lies the magic of origami: that from one initial square of paper, a multitude of coins, cards, samurai helmets, even intricate birds and flowers, can be brought to life. This sacred transformation mirrors the Buddhist teachings of 'shogyo mujo' - the transiency of worldly things; reminding us of the impermanence and interconnectedness of all things.

In conclusion, origami, in its subtle dance between hands, paper, and thought, offers an intimate exploration of the Buddhist 'Middle Path.' It gently nudges you to seek balance - between effort and ease, precision and fluidity, complexity and simplicity - reflecting the calm and equilibrium that stems from our practising mindfulness.

As you peruse this guide, turn each page like a fold, let each line settle in like a crease on paper, and let your mind embrace the art of origami in all its exquisite tranquility and profound depth. Understanding the basics leads you to unravel the rest of your journey into the beautiful world of origami. May each fold, each crease bring you closer to mindfulness and serenity.

Chapter 4. Introduction to Buddhism: The Four Noble Truths and The Eightfold Path

With its birth in the 6th century BCE in what is now known as Nepal, Buddhism centers, quite remarkably, on the teachings of Siddhartha Gautama, better known as the Buddha. "Buddha" translates to "the awakened one," a fitting epitome for the enlightened being whose profound insights into suffering, its causes, its cessation, and the path leading to its cessation, forms the basis of Buddhist philosophy.

Buddhism embraces the notion of a practical, experiential journey rather than adherence to a set of unchangeable truths. This path of personal discovery is guided by the understanding of the Four Noble Truths and the actualization of the Noble Eightfold Path.

4.1. The Four Noble Truths

The Buddha's first and most essential teaching is about the Four Noble Truths. These encompass the truth of suffering, the truth of the origin of suffering, the truth of the cessation of suffering, and the truth of the path leading to the cessation.

1. Dukkha - The Truth of Suffering

In Buddhism, "Dukkha" most commonly translates to "suffering," but it encompasses the whole range of human pain - physical or mental - from the subtle to the acute. This First Noble Truth acknowledges that suffering exists in life. There is illness, aging, and mortality. We suffer when we encounter what we dislike and when we are separated from what we cherish, reflecting the inherent unsatisfactoriness of our existence.

1. Samudaya - The Origin of Suffering

The Second Noble truth, Samudaya, refers to the cause or origin of suffering. Buddhism recognizes that we bring about our own suffering through attachment (Tanha), and ignorance (Avijja). We are attached to pleasurable experiences, material possessions, and even our self-identity. This constant clinging to transient things, inevitably leads to dissatisfaction and suffering, as everything in our world is temporary and always changing.

1. Nirodha - The End of Suffering

The Third Noble Truth presents a beacon of hope - Nirodha, the cessation of suffering. Buddhism asserts that we can end suffering by completely relinquishing attachments and desires. To eliminate suffering, we must eliminate its causes, and therein lies the possibility of liberation and the attainment of Nirvana– the ultimate state of peace and happiness.

1. Magga - The Path that Leads to the End of Suffering

The Fourth Noble Truth, Magga, provides the practical guideline for living - the Noble Eightfold Path. This path, when followed, leads to the cessation of suffering.

4.2. The Noble Eightfold Path

This path is a comprehensive guide for moral conduct, concentration, and insight obtained through wisdom; it is the actualization of Buddhist principles in routine existence. It is a middle way that avoids the extremes of self-denial and self-indulgence, leading to liberation.

1. Right Understanding (Samma Ditthi)

This refers to the understanding of things as they are, especially an intellectual grasp of the Four Noble Truths. This is the foundation for the rest of the path.

1. Right Thought (Samma Sankappa)

An individual's thoughts ultimately determine their actions. This step emphasizes the importance of compassionate and benevolent thought patterns, free from ill-will and cruelty.

1. Right Speech (Samma Vaca)

Right Speech refers to abstaining from lies, harsh language, slander, and idle chatter. It signifies communicating truthfully, kindly, helpful, and at the right time.

1. Right Action (Samma Kammanta)

This entails abstaining from taking life, stealing, and sexual misconduct. It encourages actions that show respect for the life, property, and well-being of others.

1. Right Livelihood (Samma Ajiva)

This involves earning a living in a way that does not harm or exploit others and is in line with ethical and moral principles.

1. Right Effort (Samma Vayama)

This requires diligent mental effort to develop wholesome qualities and reject unwholesome ones. This determination promotes self-discipline and self-improvement.

1. Right Mindfulness (Samma Sati)

It involves retaining awareness of the body, feelings, thoughts, and phenomena in the present moment. It encourages an unbiased observation of reality, fostering wisdom and freedom from suffering.

1. Right Concentration (Samma Samadhi)

The last step is the development of a concentrated, tranquil, and alert mind through meditation practices. This deep focus leads to a greater understanding of reality and the transient nature of all things.

While the Four Noble Truths diagnose the human condition and prescribe a remedy, The Eightfold Path serves as a therapeutic regimen to alleviate suffering. Just like in origami, the act of creating something beautiful and meaningful from raw material, Buddhism promotes the transformation of an unenlightened mind into an awakened one. And like an origami master carefully folding each crease with awareness and precision, the true practitioner aligns each step along the Eightfold Path with mindfulness and intention, moving progressively toward liberation.

Chapter 5. Mindful Paper Folding: Harnessing Zen in Each Fold

Once, Thich Nhat Hanh, a revered Vietnamese Buddhist Zen Master, shed light upon the idea of "washing dishes to wash the dishes." His intent was not so much about chore completion, but rather to emphasize the importance of being completely aware and immersed in the experience of what one is doing at the moment. The same wisdom extends to the practice of Origami, where it's not just about finishing a project, but about valuing every crease, understanding every fold, and living every moment entirely to achieve a state of Zen.

5.1. Broadening Your Horizons: Origami as a Pathway

Origami, as an art form, offers dimensions beyond the physical act of folding paper. Each transformation from a simple, undistinguished sheet to gradually complex structures mirrors life's very essence. The folds represent the challenges we face, the creases, our experiences, and the final product, our realizations. The beauty of this art lies not only in its simplicity but also in the power it lends us to introspect and meditate.

Understanding this perspective requires removing the idea of origami as an end product and refocusing on respecting it as a process. A process that demands a presence of mind - consistent and undivided. Consider every paper you fold as a cosmic map of your inner universe, where each crease, each fold represents a thought, a shift, an action, or a manifestation. By focusing on the act of folding, you immerse yourself in the creation process, cultivate mindfulness, and draw ever closer to the peaceful state known widely within Buddhism as Zen.

5.2. Building the Foundation: Simplifying the Process

To begin this practice, all you need is a piece of paper, a quiet space and an intent to focus. The paper serves as a physical entity, bringing concrete form to your thoughts. Your folds are your experiences - each uniquely personal and worth understanding.

Origami is an exercise in precision and purpose. Each fold signifies something profound – a practice of mindfulness, patient perseverance, and an embodiment of the Zen philosophy. Remember, origami is not merely an act of recreating a preconceived object, but of creating significance along the journey, reminding us of Zen Buddhism's core teachings.

5.3. Engaging Mindfully: The Act of Folding

Each fold is an event, an experience, and a step toward Zen. Like a Zen koan or riddle, it invites contemplation and introspection. Thus, the act of folding itself becomes akin to a moving meditation.

As you pick up the paper, let yourself relax into the rhythm of the process. Be aware of the sensation of the paper beneath your fingers, the hushed whisper of the movement, the evolving structure taking form. Each of these sensations calls for your undivided attention, which stimulates a better understanding of, and a deeper connection with, the present moment.

While folding, mistakes will happen. Events might not quite unfold as planned metaphorically or literally. But remember, each mistake is a lesson, a reflection of life, and is as valuable as each success. When a fold goes awry, take a deep breath. Don't give in to frustration; instead, reflect on the imperfection and see it as part of the journey rather than a hinderance. This mirrors a fundamental tenet of Zen Buddhist philosophy - embracing the imperfect and learning from it.

5.4. The Role of Reflection: Discovering Inner Peace within the Folds

An important part of the origami process is the pause between the folds. These moments of stillness serve to encourage self-reflection, lending you an opportunity to examine your progress, process your feelings, and learn from your experiences.

While in this pause, reflect inward. Consider the journey you've embarked on, the patience you've exercised, the folds you've mastered, and the enhancements you could make. This process of observation, introspection and learning parallels the Buddhist philosophy, illustrating the transformative power of introspective silence, and helping us make peace with our thought processes and emotions.

5.5. The Final Unfolding: Insightful Awareness and Meaning

Finally, as you make the last crease and glance upon your completed piece, you are not merely looking at a paper bird, lotus, or frog – but a reflection of your journey. That end product serves as a physical representation of your inner harmony, patience, mindfulness and appreciation for the process.

Each origami creation, may it be simple or intricate, symbolically represents the journey of transforming a humble sheet of paper into a work of art – not simply with your hands, but with your heart and mind, engaged in a state of focused tranquility. This simultaneously mirrors the process of transformation and awakening encouraged by Buddhist teachings.

As you end your session, sit for a moment with your creation. Reflect on the steps you took, the pleasure or difficulties you had, the mistakes you made and rectified. Like the emerging patterns on an origami piece, the twists and turns, uncertainties and victories of life tell a beautiful story that's uniquely yours.

This profound exploration into mindful paper folding invites you to look at origami not only as an art but also as a meditative practice. A tool to harness the Zen in each fold, entering into a state of serenity and calm. Remember, Origami, like life, is not about how well you move to the finish line, but about understanding and cherishing each step along the way. So, here's to the next fold – may it bring you closer to your Zen.

Chapter 6. Symbolism in Origami: Going Beyond Just Shapes

Origami, the ancient art of paper folding, bears more than just its visual appeal. It is loaded with profound symbolism that stems significant facets of Buddhist philosophy, life, and nature. Each fold, each crease, and each shape constructed have a narrative to tell; a narrative that goes beyond the physical, venturing into a space where mindfulness meets creativity, where craft becomes a meditative practice, and where the simplicity of paper transcends into the complexities of life.

6.1. Understanding the Language of Origami

Origami's essence lies not just in the destination—the final figure that manifests—but also in the journey of folds and creases that leads to that destination. It is this journey, taken with intentionality and consciousness, that constitutes the language of origami—a language that uses the silence of paper but speaks volumes about life and its many hues.

The art starts with a single, unblemished sheet of paper representing the emptiness or the 'Sunyata,' a crucial concept in Buddhist philosophy. It symbolizes the pure nature of our existence before it is marked or conditioned by experiences.

Each fold indicates a step toward shaping our experiences, our beliefs, and our identities. While some folds are gentle, suggestive of favorable situations in life, others can be harsh and challenging, reminding us of life's adversities. Yet, they are vital, for they shape the final figure just like our experiences shape us.

6.2. The Spirit of Zen in Origami

The creases that garnish the paper denote our mental impressions, our 'Sanskara,' imprinted on the canvas of our minds. Just like a fold on the paper, these impressions are often indelible and influence the subsequent folds or experiences. However, through the practice of mindfulness, akin to the careful, attentive folding of paper, we can gain control over these impressions, ensuring they lead to a beautiful form and not a distorted mess.

This is where the spirit of Zen is integrated into origami. It encourages us to be present in the moment, mindfully engaged in the process of folding, mindful of each crease being formed, akin to how we can be witness to our own impressions in the continuum of consciousness.

6.3. Origami and Impermanence

Moreover, origami teaches us the impermanence of form—a fundamental teaching in Buddhism. Despite the careful crafting, a gust of wind, a drop of water, or a moment of negligence, can bring an origami sculpture to its original form—a plain, flat piece of paper—echoing the transient nature of life, the rise and fall, the creation, and the dissolution.

6.4. Symbolic Figures and their Significance

Different origami models bear their own symbolic meaning in the realm of Buddhist teachings. An origami crane, for instance, represents peace and healing. In Japanese culture, it is said that folding a thousand paper cranes brings good fortune and wellness.

These cranes are often seen in temples and sacred spaces, providing visual sermons of peace.

An origami lotus symbolizes purity and enlightenment—a motif recurrent in various Buddhist scriptures. Notably, despite its birth in muddy waters, a lotus manages to rise and blossom above the murk, untouched. This is mirrored in the folds of an origami lotus, bearing the metaphor of enlightenment, rising beyond worldly attachments to attain inner purity.

6.5. The Enso Circle and Origami

A significant symbol in Zen Buddhism is the Enso, or the circle of emptiness and enlightenment. Even though traditional origami employs geometric folds and more angular contours, contemporary origami practitioners have explored more fluid folds to create a rendition of the Enso circle. The Enso origami model embodies the Zen philosophy of 'form is emptiness and emptiness is form,' emphasizing the deeper understanding of reality beyond superficial demarcations.

Origami is an art form steeped in symbolism and infused with philosophical ponderings. It encourages a unique alliance of mindfulness and creativity, paying homage to life's impermanence and the pursuit of enlightenment. The inherent symbolism in origami is a silent teacher, imparting wisdom not through words, but through folds, creases, and the undulating journey it takes from a flat sheet to a beautiful, multidimensional form. Going beyond just shapes, Origami evolves as a silent narrative of the human journey, embedded within the serenity of folds.

Chapter 7. Traditional Buddhist Symbols in Origami

Buddhism and Origami have been intrinsically weaved together, representing a rich tapestry of spiritual and creative expression. We embark on the exploration of traditional Buddhist symbols in Origami, delving deep into the meanings and origami interpretations of these symbols.

7.1. The Lotus Flower

One of the most enduring symbols in Buddhism, the lotus flower represents purity and enlightenment, its beauty untouched by the muddy water from which it originates.

To create an Origami lotus, start with a square piece of paper. Fold in half diagonally both ways, then fold in half into a rectangle from both directions. You should have crease lines that intersect in the center of your paper. Fold each corner into the center. Flip the paper over, then fold each corner into the center again. Fold corners into the center a third time, then gently pull out the corners from under each triangle you just made.

As you fold the lotus and see it take shape, reflect on the Buddhist teaching of our potential to rise above challenges, emerging intact and beautiful despite adversity—just like the lotus flower.

7.2. The Dharma Wheel

The Dharma wheel or Dharmachakra represents the path to enlightenment—a central tenet in Buddhism. It highlights the cyclical nature of life and the journey of spiritual awakening.

To make an origami Dharma wheel, begin with a square paper sheet. Fold the paper in half in both ways. Then fold the corners to meet in the center. Flip the paper and fold new corners into the center again. Fold the miniature square in half, and then unfold to get a cross-like crease. Fold the left and right sides towards the center using the crease. Flip it over, and voila, you have your origami Dharmachakra.

As your fingers manipulate the paper into a Dharmachakra, allow your mind to reflect on the Eightfold Path—the guide to ethical living, understanding, mindfulness and the cessation of desire and suffering it signifies.

7.3. The Eternal Knot

The Eternal Knot, also known as the Endless Knot, symbolizes the interconnectedness of all life and the endless wisdom of Buddha. It also represents the union of wisdom and compassion.

Crafting an origami eternal knot may seem complex, but with patience and focus, you can create this beautiful symbol. Begin with a rectangular piece of paper. Fold and unfold it diagonally. Fold each side towards the crease created, forming a smaller diamond shape. The intricate entwining of the paper symbolizes the complexity and interconnectedness of life and the universe.

7.4. The Bodhi Tree

The Bodhi tree holds significant importance as Gautama Buddha is believed to have attained enlightenment under this tree. Making a tree from paper draws parallels with the deep roots of Buddhist teachings and the enlightenment that unfolds just like a well-nourished tree.

To fold a Bodhi tree, start with a green square paper. Fold it into half diagonally, horizontally, and vertically to create intersecting creases.

Use these creases to form a preliminary base. Fold the sides towards the center crease and then fold the top triangle down. In the end, make creases for leaves and branches to give it a realistic tree shape.

7.5. The Buddha

To fold in the image of Buddha is to fold in the essence of enlightenment, peace, and spiritual awakening. It is a worthwhile challenge to create an origami Buddha.

For a simple Buddha, start with a square piece. Create a waterbomb base and then fold the upper and lower corners to the center. Further, fold the figure into half, and then make a squash fold. Finally, make a couple of inside reverse folds for hands and head.

Each fold represents aspects of Buddha's teachings. When the form is complete, contemplate on inner peace and enlightenment—the vital goal in Buddhism.

By bringing to life these essential symbols of Buddhism through origami, we bridge the gap between physical creativity and spiritual contemplation. These paper renditions serve as physical manifestations of the philosophical ideologies that they represent. They amplify the power of mindfulness by engaging your mind and hands and offer an innovative pathway for deeper understanding of Buddhism teachings. Experience the serenity that comes with each fold, and enrich your journey towards enlightenment.

Therefore, engaging in the practice of folding traditional Buddhist symbols in origami fosters a multi-dimensional comprehension and appreciation of Buddhist philosophy. As the symbol takes shape between your fingers, may the essence of these profound teachings web their profound wisdom into your life.

Chapter 8. Practical Exercises: Creating Mindfulness through Origami

Origami is traditionally associated with Japanese culture, but it resonates strongly with the concepts at the heart of Buddhism, particularly mindfulness and meditation. Through the gentle folds of paper and the quiet focus needed to complete each creation, one embarks on a unique path of mental clarity and serenity.

Before we delve into practical exercises, it's important to remember that the aim is not merely to finish the origami models, but also to remain present throughout the process. The act of creasing, folding, and shaping paper can unlock a sense of inner calm and awareness that serves as a grounding mindfulness technique.

8.1. Gathering Your Materials

Start by assembling all the necessary materials to begin your origami journey. Although origami paper, or "kami," is most traditional, you don't need to be particular about the type of paper, especially as a beginner. Any paper that folds easy and holds a crease will suffice.

You may want to create a serene, quiet space in your home where you can engage in this practice undisturbed. Set the stage with a simple, clean table, adequate lighting, and perhaps even inspiring elements like a candle, incense, or calming music.

8.2. Mindful Origami Ritual

Start developing a mindful origami ritual:

1. Begin by washing your hands. This is more than mere hygiene; it symbolizes cleansing yourself of any worries or disruptive thoughts.

2. Sit comfortably and maintain a good posture. This helps keep your energy level stable and contributes to your overall focus.

3. Take a few moments to connect with your breath. Conscious breathing is one of the core elements of mindfulness and Buddhist meditation.

4. Finally, pick up a piece of paper and observe it. Take note of its texture, its weight, and its color.

Once you feel centered, you can start your origami practice.

8.3. Dive into your first Origami

The traditional origami crane is a quintessential model for beginners. As you follow these steps, remember to focus on each fold, each crease, allowing all other thoughts to naturally drift away.

1. Start with a perfectly square piece of paper. If you're not using traditional origami paper, simply cut a square piece from the material of your choice.

2. Fold the square diagonally to create a triangle. **continued**

Work with the triangle, making folds to slowly morph its form into that of a crane. Don't rush through this – let every fold be a mindful practice. If your mind begins to wander, gently guide your attention back to the paper and your hands.

Origami is an art that originates from a deep place of mindfulness and patience, so be guided by the process rather than the result. After all, Buddhism teaches us that the journey is more important than the destination.

8.4. Variations and Exploration

Once you've become adept at the crane, explore other traditional models like the boat, the butterfly, or the lotus. Each model presents unique folds and creases, challenging you to remain mindful and focused.

You may also try 'Modular Origami', a technique where multiple identical pieces of paper are folded into units which are then assembled into a complex geometric or even floral shape. This will require further patience and focus, leading to a more advanced mindfulness practice.

8.5. Reflection and Insight

After each origami session, take a moment to reflect on what you've created – not just the tangible paper forms, but also the inner calm and clarity. Just as we transform a simple piece paper into a complex shape, the practice of origami helps in the transformation of a restless mind into a state of deep tranquility.

Moreover, each origami model can be seen as a symbol of Buddhist teachings. For example, the origami crane, which symbolizes peace and longevity in Japanese culture, can also serve as a reminder of the peace and longevity of the mind that we strive for in Buddhist practice.

8.6. Closing the Origami Practice

After completing your origami and reflection, slowly wind down. Clean your space, show gratitude for the calm and focus you've achieved, and be gentle with yourself as you transition from this place of calm back to your daily activities.

The true value of the origami practice lies not in the finished product but in the journey of creating it. The intentional and attentive folding, breath by breath, fold by fold, takes you on a journey within yourself, offering insights about your mind and deepening your understanding of the Buddhist philosophy.

This mindful and meditative practice draws us closer to ourselves, helping us embody the essence of the Buddhist philosophy: awakening to the present moment with compassionate awareness and wisdom.

Chapter 9. Origami and Buddhist Philosophy: Lessons in Impermanence and Non-Attachment

As the ancient art of paper folding, origami has taken many forms and absorbed distinct meanings since its birth in Japan more than a millennium ago. Similarly, Buddhism has a wealth of wisdom to teach about the nature of existence and the path to enlightenment. A nexus between these two, seemingly disparate, disciplines brings forth powerful insights that can illuminate the understanding of our lives, the world, and ourselves. Most notably, origami and Buddhism express shared lessons about two fundamental notions, impermanence and non-attachment.

9.1. Impermanence in Origami and Buddhism

Origami serves as a profound metaphor for impermanence. A piece of paper, while static and two-dimensional in its original state, undergoes a process of transformation when touched by an origami enthusiast's hands. With each fold, the paper morphs into something different, something new, mirroring the ever-changing nature of existence.

Buddhist philosophy underscores this principle: all conditioned existence is transient. Life is characterized by a constant state of flux – birth and death, beginning and ending, gain and loss. This is the reality of impermanence or 'annica' in Pali, one of the core teachings of Buddha.

An origami creation serves as a poignant reminder of this truth of life. It embodies the journey from creation to cessation, from existence to non-existence. The initial shape of the paper fades into irrelevance as it assumes a new identity, then another, and yet another, through an endless process of becoming and unbecoming – just like us, in our terrestial journey.

Yet, as evocative as an origami sculpture, life's impermanence does not imply nihilism but instead encourages a deeper appreciation of the present moment and an abiding reverence for life's transient journeys.

9.2. Harnessing Creativity Through Impermanence

By folding, unfolding, and refolding the paper, origami allows its creator to experience firsthand the ceaseless change that is a core tenet of Buddhist philosophy. Our shared journey with the origami paper teaches us to embrace the freedom and creativity that impermanence brings while simultaneously confronting the inevitability of transience.

The ephemeral nature of origami beckons us gently to the metaphorical drawing board. The pristine paper holds infinite potential - a crane, a lotus, a dragon, or any creation bound only by the constraints of imagination and dexterity. This is the nature of origami, and, metaphorically, our existence. Confronted with the blank canvas of life, we are free to create, to shift course, to embrace change, encapsulating the Buddhist spirit of adaptation and evolution.

9.3. Non-Attachment in Origami and Buddhism

The practice of both origami and Buddhism also entails the study of non-attachment, or 'anicca'. Non-attachment in Buddhism refers to letting go or relinquishing one's grip on the self, possessions, experiences, and the outcome of our actions. For how can we hold onto something in a world that is intrinsically fluid and in a perpetual state of flux?

Origami, with its focus on process over product, embodies this perfectly. An origamist engaged in the art form pays deep attention to every fold and crease, immersing fully in the present moment, thereby practicing mindfulness – a cornerstone of meditation, itself a core practice in Buddhism.

In origami, the art lies not in the end product, but in the process–the meditative action of folding, the quiet focus, the connection between hand and paper. Once an origami sculpture is complete, it is set aside, detached, let go, much like a practitioner of Buddhism who forsakes attachment in search of enlightenment.

9.4. Practicing Non-Attachment through Origami

Non-attachment is taught and practiced through the act of gifting or disposing of the origami creation once complete – an act that symbolizes release. One of the popular customs in the world of origami is Senbazuru, a string of a thousand origami cranes. Created as a labor of love, these strings are often gifted or left at sacred shrines. In this, we see a beautiful act of practicing non-attachment.

The process of origami forces us to confront attachment – to our creations, our ideas, even our mistakes. It encourages the development of a gentle flexibility and resilience, the ability to let go, and start again – a valuable lesson to carry into our daily life.

9.5. Origami, Buddhism, and the Journey Beyond

In drawing these parallels between origami and Buddhist teachings, we find a path that uses the simplicity of folded paper to unfold complex philosophical teachings about impermanence and non-attachment. Origami teaches us, in tactile and visual ways, to embrace change and to release attachment – two lessons that sit at the heart of Buddhist principles.

Origami, while being an art, is also a mirror reflecting profound truths about existence as understood in the Buddhist lens. As an origami model evolves from a planar sheet to a multi-faceted sculpture, we map our own journey from a state of unconscious existence to enlightened self-awareness.

The practice of origami holds within its folds a world of serene reflection, tranquility, and deep learning, an art form taking you gently towards the doors of Buddhist teachings and wisdom. It is a testament that our journey toward enlightenment can begin and continue to unfurl from something as simple and unpretentious as a sheet of paper.

Chapter 10. Inspirational Stories: Testimonials from Buddhist Origami Practitioners

The beautiful and humbling world of Buddhist Origami is rich with transformative stories. Each story reveals a unique journey and a profound transformation, much like each origami fold manifesting a unique shape. Here, we share some of these heartfelt testimonials from practitioners of all walks of life, and their transformative experiences with Buddhist Origami.

10.1. A Monastic Origami Journey

Kōzan, a robed monk currently residing in Japan, found his pathway to Buddhism through the intricate art of origami. He recalls initially stumbling upon origami during his childhood. His hands, which felt most comfortable in prayer, soon found a different kind of devotion within the folds of paper.

"I was drawn towards origami as a medium of self-expression. Then, I began exploring Buddhist teachings and quickly found a deeper, more profound connection. Origami, just like Buddhism, encourages us to construct and deconstruct, to reach a more profound understanding of our transient reality. The attention one gives to each crease, the respect towards the paper, is no different from cultivating mindfulness in our interactions with the world," Kōzan shares.

Over the years, Kōzan has trained himself to imbue specific meanings into his origami creations. He painstakingly modelled the "Lotus Sutra," a significant text in Buddhism, using a single piece of paper. A metaphor for the Buddha-nature inherent in all beings, the delicate origami lotus helps Kōzan to remind himself of the purity and potential within him and others.

10.2. From Turmoil to Tranquility: An Urban Soldier's Tale

Edward, a retired soldier from the U.S, recounts his tale of transformation, beginning with the chaos and stress of combat and culminating in the peaceful practice of origami. Post-retirement, his world was fraught with disquiet and discomfort as he battled post-traumatic stress disorder (PTSD) and struggled to readjust to civilian life.

"I used to wake up with nightmares of explosions and gunfire. My life was cluttered with remembrances of war," he admits. His encounter with Buddhist Origami, however, provided him with a peaceful means to combat his inner turmoil.

Edward discovered origami during a group therapy session. He fell in love instantly with the quiet concentration needed to transform a bare sheet into a beautiful object. Learning about its connection with Buddhist practice added a layer of depth to this simple but unique art.

"The act of folding paper offered a distinct, focused calmness. I started to devote more time to learning Buddhist teachings, and soon, the unsettling recollections began to dissipate. The simple, meditative act of folding paper helped bridge the chasm between my past and present." Edward's expression softens as he fondly folds a sheet of paper into a mandala, an embodiment of the universe in Buddhism, a symbol of his inner journey to peace.

10.3. Birds of Hope: An Entrepreneur's Road to Emotional Healing

Anoushka, a tech mogul from India, was living the dream of many - a successful start-up, wealth, and influence. Yet, amid the fast-paced life and stress of her entrepreneurial journey, she lost sight of herself. A swift rise to success masked her deep-seated anxiety and loneliness.

"I felt trapped, burdened by the responsibility of my dreams," Anoushka remembers. She sought therapy to help her handle these weighty emotions. It was here that she found an unlikely solution — Buddhist Origami.

Initially sceptical, Anoushka started folding origami cranes, a sign of hope and healing in Japanese culture, while concurrently exploring Buddhist teachings. She found in these folds an unexpected sense of calm and freedom.

"The more cranes I folded, the more I experienced tranquility. Voluntarily surrendering control, working with my hands while my mind remained free, helped me with a sense of release. This reciprocity between folding and Buddhist teachings helped me look for solutions, not outside, but within myself."

The testimonials above provide glimpses into a variety of individual journeys – each unique and transformative. The common thread binding them all is the art of origami and its inherent Buddhist principles. By gently folding mindfulness and patience into each action, these individuals have learned to reshape not just paper, but their own lives, signifying the profound impact of Buddhist Origami on our quest for inner peace and self-realization.

Chapter 11. Embracing the Journey: Fostering Your Own Buddhist Origami Practice

As you turn a flat piece of paper into a three-dimensional sculpture through the art of origami, you engage in a profound interaction with the principles of the material world—symmetry, equilibrium, and transformation. The process of folding and unfolding echoes philosophical truths inherent in Buddhism, namely the concepts of impermanence, non-self and interdependent arising. As simple as they may seem, these similar transitions represent an easy way to focus the mind and attain peace, while simultaneously acting as symbols of bigger, more complex Buddhist teachings.

11.1. Engaging with the Basics of Origami

Before you can start folding paper into meaningful shapes, you must first understand the fundamentals of origami. These basics form the foundation of the art form, much like the Four Noble Truths are fundamental to Buddhist practice.

An origami project begins with a single square sheet, untarnished and uncreased. This untouched paper symbolizes the beginner's mind in Buddhism, which values openness and a readiness to learn. As you fold the paper, you transition from potential to the actual, crafting order from chaos. Every fold is a step on the journey of creation, an evolution from simplicity to complexity.

But the beauty of origami lies not merely in the finished product, but in the process. Each fold must be executed with detail, accuracy, and patience. Mindfulness permeates this practice, as each crease demands your full attention. The physical action of folding translates to a mental letting go of external distractions and a refocusing of your concentration on the present moment.

11.2. The Symbolism in Different Origami Figures

Familiar with the fundamentals of origami folding, you're now ready to explore the meanings behind specific pieces. In addition to being aesthetic creations, most origami models carry deeper messages that resonate with Buddhist principles.

For instance, the origami crane, a symbol of peace and longevity in Asian cultures, is often linked to the Buddhist teaching of practicing patience and radiating kindness. A lotus flower, an iconic symbol of enlightenment in Buddhism, can also be intricately folded out of paper, representing a journey from ignorance to wisdom. The transformation of paper to a lotus speaks about the journey of enlightenment, emerging from the depths of hardship into a state of purity and peace.

These are just two examples of many. The joy lies in unearthing the symbolism of each origami model and seeing its reflection in Buddhist ethos.

11.3. The Impact of Nature in Origami and Buddhism

Nature plays a central role in both Buddhism and origami, serving as inspiration and symbol. The tranquility and simplicity of natural elements is embodied in the practice of origami, where a single square sheet of paper can transform into a complex and beautiful object mimicking a natural form.

The very act of folding paper mimics the natural processes of transformation—flower buds blooming, leaves changing colors, cocoon transforming into a butterfly. It's a simplistic representation of natural evolutionary processes, reminding us of the ever-changing nature of life, an essential Buddhist teaching.

11.4. Meditative Folding: Achieving Mindfulness through Origami

Just like practicing Buddhism, folding origami can be a form of meditation. Each fold is a mindful movement—conscious, purposeful, and completely engaging—and requires a focused mind.

As you work with paper, embracing its fragility and respecting its patience, you learn to slow down, observing each movement in the now. With each crease, your mind unclutters, and you allow yourself to rest in the present moment, fostering a state of calm alertness.

By transforming origami into a mindful, meditative practice, you can foster your spirit of Zen, affirm life's impermanence, cultivate awareness and compassion, and make a real step towards your own understanding of the Buddhist philosophy.

11.5. Each Fold Counts: A Lesson in Patience and Persistence

When practicing origami, it is necessary to maintain a serene equilibrium, to focus unwaveringly on each fold and to persevere until the final figure emerges. This practice teaches patience and diligence, virtues revered in Buddhism.

Every time you meet an intricate fold, you might feel tested, but pressing on with patience and attention brings valuable lessons. Indeed, embracing the journey is not about quick achievement but sits in the heart of experiencing each intricate fold, each moment of your existence.

By fostering the practice of origami, you embark on a journey that mirrors life, filled with ups and downs, challenges and rewards, complexities and simplicities. You learn to meet each moment exactly as it is, accepting, letting go, and remaining centered—a path that Buddhism encourages all followers to pursue.

11.6. When a Fold Unfolds: Lessons in Impermanence

In Buddhism, the concept of impermanence tells us that nothing in life is permanent; all phenomena are in a state of flux. This very principle is imprinted in every fold and unfold of origami.

An origami model, once folded, can be unfolded back into the original sheet of paper. This returning to the original form highlights the transient nature of all things, a potent lesson in emptiness and impermanence.

Each time you fold a piece of paper, you transform its identity, but the essence—the paper—remains the same. It is an expression of the impermanence and constant change in the world around us and within us. By reflecting on this, you gain deeper insights into the Buddhist philosophy of life.

In essence, when you embrace origami as a meditative practice, you not only foster serenity and creativity, but you also get an intimate glimpse into the principles of Buddhism. So, pick up a piece of paper and let yourself be guided through a journey of mindful exploration and philosophical discovery; you'll find simplicity on one side and universality on the other, all manifest in the palm of your hand.